Editor, English-language edition
Richard Pierce

Designer
Gigi Schiemann

© 2002 Mondadori Electa S.p. A., Milano

Mondadori Libri Illustrati

First edition: June 2002

Second edition: February 2004

www.librimondadori.it

ISBN 88-435-8182-1

Printed in February 2004

by Artes Gràficas Toledo S.A.U.

Printed in Spain

Venice Sketchbook

Huck Scarry's

Venice Sketchbook

MONDADORI

INTRODUCTION

"Nothing can be said here that has not been said before."

Mary McCarthy,
Venice Preserved, 1956

*I*ndeed, what hasn't already been written? What more could one possibly paint?

And yet, though so familiar in my mind's eye, Venice never fails to amaze me. Every day is like the very first. I just can't get blasé.

I have searched for an analogy to Venice. Oddly, I found it in a flea market: You know in advance exactly what you can expect to find, you may even be familiar with the various stalls. Yet, as you browse, something you never expected catches the corner of your eye. You stop, intrigued, and pick it up. Which is just how I collected the pages of this book.

The day's wash at Cannaregio.

From the beginning, to my editor's despair, I worked without any pre-established outline. It was in vain that I had tried to plan my first working days. For it was Venice that decided what I would or would not see. If I set out under sun, she made it rain. If I determined a route, she led me down a wrong calle. If I had a goal, then square in my path an unwanted, unwished-for, unyielding subject snared me, and held me back from what I originally went out to draw. It took some sensitivity, and luck, to give up, give in, and see it.

Which is why I paid no attention to the quotation above, nor concerned myself that Venice has already been treated by the most talented hands. Surely, one's subject matters less than just how you see it, and can describe it. I have striven, not to make a good book about Venice, just a good book.

I have heard it said: What is good, will always be new.

Closed stalls, early morning.

CANALS

The first time I took a boat ride through the back canals was some time after I had already memorized my pedestrian itineraries through the city. As the boat weaved its way through unfamiliar passages, all the landmarks I had learned were thrown in disorder. Churches and palaces and squares that I knew, would appear by surprise, and far from where I thought they belonged.

Of course, what I was discovering is something unique to Venice: The city is built with two distinct networks of communication. Streets to get about on foot, and canals for transport by boat. The two have very little use for each other, and apart from short stretches along a fondamenta, usually only meet up at right angles, saluting each other briefly at a bridge. The Grand Canal severs the street network right in two. Until the last century, the only place to cross from one side of Venice to the other without a boat, was over the Rialto bridge. This is why, each time I cross the bridge, I can't repress doing something childish: Halfway over, at the top, I stop. From where I stand, ahead and behind, spread both halves of all of Venice's streets. Below me, and to my right and left, is the Grand Canal, from whose edges are laced all of Venice's canals. I stomp on the middlemost paving stone, and have found the center of Venice.

Rio S. Giovanni Laterano, Castello.

14

Winter

The water level is extremely low. The newspaper announces -80 cm from the mean sea level will be attained today. Many of the narrow canals are dry, and the small boats moored in them lie on a bed of shiny black mud. Hopefully, fireboats and ambulances won't be needed today.

Water traffic below my window, normally very busy, has all but stopped. I watch a delivery boat hesitantly turn the corner. "Clank!" snaps the propeller, biting the muddy bottom. The skipper switches off the engine, lifts the rudder out of its seat, and with an oar punts his craft along. How fragile this city's existence! What faith in the sea! A meter too much water: no pedestrians. A meter too little: no boats. Either way, and it's not much, and there would be no Venice.

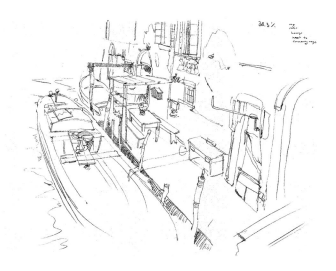

The traghetto landing at Santa Maria del Giglio.

16

Morning on the Grand Canal, at Campo San Vito.

A Reflection

I am up and out very early to get ahead of the midday heat. These past few days, on my walks along the canals, my eyes have been drawn to the play of colors on the water, under the sun.

This morning, I place myself in the shade of a small bridge, at water's edge. While I work, a friend passes and notices me. I can sense a bit of surprise at the sight of bright splashes of color on my paper. "Oh, I thought you might be drawing those wonderful boats over there," she says.

I had not previously noticed any boats nearby, but indeed, turning right around to the direction she indicated, were moored a yellow regata gondola and a lavender one, shouting out for my attention. "That's the trouble with this place," I replied. "Wherever I work, I feel I should be painting what is just behind my back."

Rio degli Ognissanti

Venice is a notorious trap for painters. I have to smile every time I see one on a bridge, turning out yet another quaint view of some narrow canal: so picturesque, hackneyed, and boring! The challenge of painting Venice is in finding unusual subject matter, in seeing familiar things in an original way. So I rarely stand on bridges. But here is an exception: the bridge over Rio degli Ognissanti. This canal is wide, and its spaciousness gives one the feeling of a small harbor. The little houses and Gesuati church form a delicate composition. The afternoon sun on the warm walls is spilling wonderful colors into the canal. But the light will soon fade, and I have to decide quickly when to stop. Arrives a jovial Frenchman on holiday with easel, paper, and conversation. He studies what I'm doing, then sets up his easel beside me. That settles it!

Rio degli Ognissanti, Dorsoduro.

BRIDGES

*I*f I ever have a bulky load to carry through town on my caddie, from a suitcase to bottles of Prosecco, I plan my route first, so as not to cross one bridge too many. And our neighborhood supermarket will make home deliveries, but no farther than three bridges away. It's that the steps are at odds with the wheels. New visitors trailing wheeled luggage, and unfamiliar with Venice's bridges, get a first taste of this as they step out of the railway station and meet a monumental, and unavoidable, flight of steps. Here I have watched some novice attempts to get a caddie down. Should it go ahead? Should it go behind? Invariably, halfway down, the load reels over with a thud, and the first lesson is learned: Both wheels must go over the steps in unison!

Far back in the city's murky beginnings, while settlements were rising on the low-lying banks of mud, there must have been a struggle for supremacy between hooved-and-wheeled conveyances and those on the water. Any flat bridge thrown across a canal forceably cuts it off to boats. Steep, arched bridges, which let the boats slip under, nonetheless kept wheeled vehicles from crossing. Happily, the boats prevailed. But I can't help thinking, had Venice's foundations stood but a meter higher, the bridges would have been flatter, and wheels – eventually

Early morning, Rio di San Lorenzo, Castello.

22

motorized – would rule the city's
streets today.

So, as I cross a canal, my arms
straining while my caddie bangs
angrily at each step, I still have a
grateful thought for the many little
bridges of Venice.

Built in a variety of materials and
styles, from wood to brick and stone,
to iron, it is surprising how so many
different bridge designs fit gracefully

Rialto bridge.

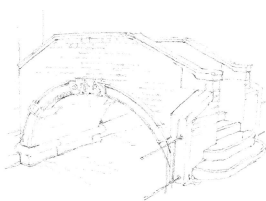

into the city. There are scarcely two alike, each has its own character, and it is rare to find one that doesn't please the eye. Below is the last bridge in Venice without railings, *Fondamenta di San Felice, Cannaregio.* Above, a little iron bridge, and one in brick, at *San Stae.*

The Bridge of Sighs.

26

Underfoot

One of the delights here is the variety of materials one's feet encounter throughout the day. Indoors: The mirror-smooth "pavimento alla veneziana" of crushed marble and lime, and cool marble staircases.

Outside: An irregular, wobbly brick courtyard, wooden docks and gangways, metal decks on vaporettos, and of course, everywhere, those rectangular, grey paving stones.

In Venice, no matter where you are, off they go, lined up one before the other, marching away down a calle, or across a campo, as far as the next bridge. Like the bridges, these stones house all the city's utilities. Sometimes you can see workmen making repairs to pipes or wires, squatting on the ground, a neat pile of paving stones stacked nearby. It only requires a crowbar to lift out just the necessary stones to get to where they want. And once the work is finished, the stones (numbered with chalk) will fit right back in their place. You will rarely hear a jackhammer in Venice.

The stones also hold a secret. When the sun shines they look drab, and uniformly grey. But when it rains and the water varnishes them, they glow with rich, subtle colors: Moss green, violet, ocher, blue, or russet.

And when it rains, it is a good idea to keep your eye on them, for they are imps. Their uneven surface often unexpectedly dips, making for fine puddles, and well-soaked shoes.

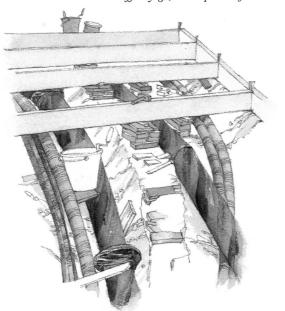

The Ponte del Vin under repair.

FACADES

With its curve of seats running round the half-moon railing, sheltered under an ample roof, the stern of the vaporetto is a floating veranda. I sit here very happily, leaning against the railing, with the swish of pale green water skimming by my feet. The vaporetto's propeller beats ponderously below the deck, and as the veranda is pushed along, the Grand Canal unravels behind it like a seemingly endless green ribbon. And two parades – one on each side – of the most wonderful buildings proceed steadily past me. I will never really accept that all these houses should have been built here: not beside, but IN the water. Nor that anything like them is not to be seen anywhere else. The richness and variety of details never lets your eyes relax. My attention jumps from a quatrefoil window, to a sculpted head, up to a chimney pot, across crumbling plaster, hops along some brick crenellations and speckled roofs of tiles.

I lean heavier on the veranda railing and think that every single thing I see was brought here from somewhere else. Even the very foundations of Venice are imported.

Hidden from view, beneath water and mud, stand forests of wooden pilings which once grew in the hills of Cadore. Bricks and roof tiles were fired from clay, brought from the neighboring mainland. The white istrian stone was carved from quarries across the Adriatic, while the pink and ocher marble come from Verona. Sand was brought from the Brenta river, and all the grey paving

Riva degli Schiavoni.

stones originate from the Eugean Hills near Padua. All assembled here, in this corrosive environment of salt, by the hands of men.

And of course, every article of day-to-day living had to be brought to Venice as well. Flour, grain, vegetables, cloth, leather. Everything. Not even drinking water escapes the list. For in spite of the cistern basins built to catch rainwater, there was never enough to go around. And so a guild of boatmen known as "acquaroli" regularly rowed across the lagoon to a branch of the Brenta to bring Venice water to drink.

Exodus

This is the most wonderful city to live in. What a pleasure to get about everywhere on foot, or by boat. To greet friends in the street, and not worry about where to park. Without motorized traffic, children are given a sense of independence they could have nowhere else today. And, happily, serious crimes remain a rarity here.

Yet, I regularly see transport boats on the Grand Canal, piled up with furniture, cardboard boxes, potted plants, and rolled-up carpets, moving. And they are always moving UP the Grand Canal, in the direction of the mainland. There are less than 70,000 inhabitants living here now, and next year there will be even fewer. The reasons are easy to find.

First, it is nearly impossible to find a reasonably priced apartment and rents are high. Secondly, outside of the tourism sector and related professions, there is simply no work to be found here. So for many young Venetians, emigration is the only solution.

This is the most important problem the city faces today, for without an indigenous population, Venice will soon be no more than a sterile theme park for tourists.

When billions can be found for megaprojects like giant dams against floodwaters from the sea, shouldn't funds first be spent to halt the drain of Venice's inhabitants? While I don't pretend to know the solutions, I can imagine some exceptional initiatives: A tax reduction for residents, as an incentive to stay. Encourage artists, professionals and businesses in the service sector to settle here, offering them reasonable housing and workspace in the numerous buildings standing sadly vacant in the city and neighboring islands.

From the vaporetto landing at San Tomà, the sweep of palaces on the Grand Canal.

Stay tuned

They stand against the sky, like scraggly body hair sprouting from the crusty tile roofs. There is scarcely a house which hasn't grown at least one, so today there is no Venetian rooftop view that doesn't include a good assortment of TV antennas. Sure, they are hideous, but there they are! Here is one, for instance, bending with interest to whisper to his neighbor. There is another, standing rigidly erect, bristling from top to bottom with spiked defenses. And funnily, a good number seem to have caught airborne barbecue grills on their spits.

What more can I say, except that I have found a practical use for these aluminum eyesores: Should I lose my sense of direction while walking through town, I need only lift my eyes to the antennas. Unfailingly, they all point me the way toward Mestre. Which comes as no surprise.

The view from my kitchen.

36

Smokestacks

*Truly characteristic of Venice's skyline
are the chimney stacks.*

*Most typical are the cone-shaped ones
that look to me as if they were
unbolted from American wood-burning
locomotives. The resemblance is no
coincidence, for the stacks of both the
locomotives and Venetian chimneys
were designed to arrest any errant live
sparks. Many chimneys have now lost
their stacks, which have been replaced
by a simple stone slab on top. But
you can detect where the stack should
be from the ring of protruding bricks
circling the chimney's neck.*

*The variety of Venetian chimneys is
delightful. I am particularly fond of
the helmet-shaped one on the roof of
the Mint, as well as another on the
Giudecca, resembling a twisted
stack of cards. On a brief afternoon
walk through town, with my nose
to the sky, here is what I was
able to collect.*

N. A.

"Numeri Anagrafici" is the great big name given to those tiny little numbers painted over every doorway in Venice. In this town of curiosities, street names are used almost exclusively in speech, and only to denote a location. A street is not an address. You wouldn't write one on an envelope. The number over your door is your address. Each "sestiere" of the city has its own list, starting with number one, and running upwards until all the doors have been exhausted.

38

Wellheads

Unable to drill for water on the islands of the lagoon, the Venetians devised a rather unusual well to catch and filter rainwater. Wellheads can be seen in most of the squares in Venice.

This one stands in Campo S. Boldo, near S. Stae. The wellhead is actually the top of a cistern reservoir dug underneath the square whose edges can be imagined from the istrian stone paving design. Dug some five meters deep, sealed watertight, and filled with sand, these reservoirs received run-off rainwater through little gutter holes pierced in the pavement. Filtered through the meters of sand, the collected water could then be brought up by rope through the wellhead.

Thus, what Nature failed to provide the Venetians, they recreated artificially for themselves. And note the little birdbath thoughtfully carved into the foundation!

Campo San Boldo, Santa Croce.

40

Palazzo Barbaro

I once saw an artist in Venice using a ruler while making a drawing. I wondered what he could possibly be looking at!

There is scarcely a building in this city with a straight line. Each one has a slight twist to it, a sagging shoulder.

The undulating rooflines express perfectly the soft, aquatic foundations these buildings rise from. Which makes them a delight to draw.

This was, for a time, the view from my desk, across the Grand Canal to Palazzo Barbaro.

Palazzo Barbaro.

Palazzo Contarini Corfu.

Meow

One meets lots of animals here. Pigeons, of course, and seagulls cawing to be fed in the wintertime. Sometimes you hear a canary singing from its cage, placed in an open window. Swallows scream and whistle about the rooftops. And scurrying around the damp foundations, at water's edge, live the "pantegane," Venice's robust water rats.

This is precisely why, no matter where you are in Venice, you will never be lonely for cats. They are everywhere. On stoops, in shopwindows, in baskets placed on the sidewalk, in boats.

Just off Strada Nuova, near the Ghetto, there is always a good number of cats lying about. When I went out to draw them, I soon understood why. Nearby, there is a wide, red door marked *Cat Refuge*, next to which is an open window where the cats can enter and exit.

Above a narrow slit carved in the door is tacked a sign: *Offering for Cats*.

The cats looked all pretty skinny, so I pushed through some lire.

One cat had lost an ear, another an eye. While I was drawing, one of them rubbed incessantly back and forth between my ankles.

Then I followed one of these cats on a walk into the Ghetto. For a moment he stopped, and crouched to pounce on a fly. I worked with my brush, and then heard something slap on the pavement between us. The cat was on it in an instant, for it was edible. You see, in Venice, just for cats, it rains chicken.

Here and there, in the corner of a campo, you will find a little cat chalet, built as shelter for the winter.

ST. MARK'S SQUARE

I cross a bridge, traverse a dark passage, and enter the morning sunshine of Piazza San Marco. My eye catches the sight of tables and chairs being eaten by the crawling shadow of the Campanile. I set down my stool and hastily begin brushing in the impression.

Then a slick, groomed head bends over my paper.

"Buongiorno, Collega!" says the head, "I am a Pittore, too! I see you are making an acquaforte."

"No, an acquarello," I reply.

He waves his newspaper. "Acquarello, acquaforte! It's all the same thing, no?"

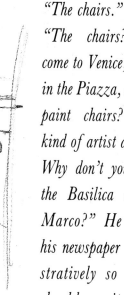

I don't reply. There is a pause, but he still hovers overhead. "I don't understand what it is you are painting," he goes on.

"The chairs."

"The chairs?! You come to Venice, you sit in the Piazza, and you paint chairs? What kind of artist are you? Why don't you paint the Basilica di San Marco?" He waves his newspaper demonstratively so that I should see it. After further advice to watch my perspective, he finally goes away, shaking both his slick head and newspaper.

It was hard going, but I got my picture.

The Piazzetta.

46

Menù turistico
Trattoria
Vaporetto
Pizzeria
Two, Tronchetto.
Ferrovia
Francobollo
Cartolina
Marco Polo.
Gelato
Rialto
Murano
Coperto,
Lira
Birra
Open
Aperto.
Kodak
Fuji
It's a
Sony.
Gondola
Gondola
Bitte,
Signori!

The Procuratie Vecchie, San Marco.

Caffè Quadri

Early morning sun pours through the arcade of the Procuratie Vecchie, aglow with the golden shadow of the lowered canvas curtains. It's like a quiet cloister ambulatory.

But not for long. At nine o'clock thunderous store shutters are thrown up, beckoning herds of tourists. A blazing pink thigh bumps into my board. Ice cream wobbles at my shoulder. White, northern feet in loose sandals repeatedly trip over a paving stone just in front of me.

Outside, the Caffè's curtains bake crisply in the sun. Here I should be allowed more elbow room. But wary about being interrupted again, I brush in the lot quickly, and at risk. I'm lucky, and get just what I want.

Caffè Quadri.

Piazzetta

Sharp, white morning sun fills the sky of the Bacino. It reflects off the Sansovino library into the still damp and shaded Piazzetta.

A motonave has pulled in from the Lido, and commuters from the island pass through here on their way to work. What finer way to begin one's day!

The lion normally perched atop one of the granite pillars of the Piazzetta has taken to wing. Away for restoration.

Early morning, Piazzetta.

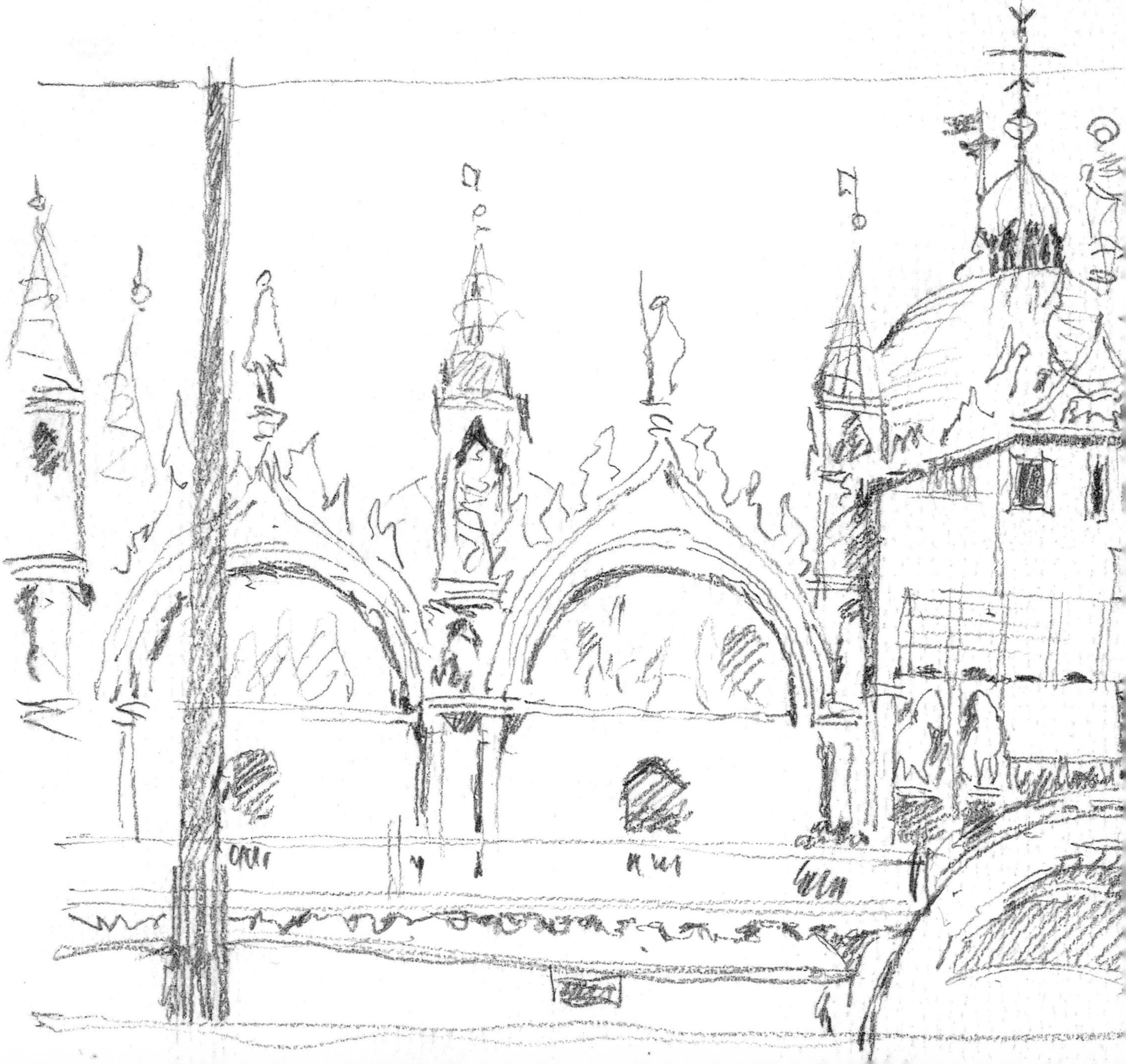

53

54

Under the cupolas

*Inside the basilica, I feel like an
insect within the petals of an exotic
flower. The minute geometry, found
everywhere in Nature, is also on
everything you see in here!*

The cupolas of St. Mark's.

Pigeons

They are not particularly attractive, they do not sing, and they are messy. Yet I always come upon a little pile of breadcrumbs left on a bridge, or find a bowl of water placed at the foot of a fountain. A birdbath has been built in front of the tugs on Riva Schiavoni, and another forms part of the wellhead beside St. Mark's. And it is not rare, on a winter day, to see a grown man crushing up hard bread under his foot. Why are Venetians so fond of their pigeons? Of course, what I remember most of my first visit here, aged ten, was the thrill of feeding them myself. And I'm sure it is no different for many of the day-trippers today in St. Mark's Square. Puffed-out and pompous, or tattered and feather-bare, these birds are every bit a piece of this city. And their blotchy grays and whites are perfectly matched to the weather-beaten facades of the Procuratie on which they roost.

The flagmasts outside the basilica.

MASKS

This morning a slight fog is keeping the air damp and nippy, and the paving stones of Piazza San Marco are slow to give up their shiny, wet polish of the night. A pale sun attempts to pierce the foggy veil, imparting a silver glow to the air.

This is the last day of Carnival. The square is still, and the only movement is the lazy wave from ragged cloth that hangs as a backdrop to a theater stage. Vendors' stalls stand veiled under cotton umbrellas and sheets, ghostly white. I set down my stool and draw.

Pigeons strut jerkily around my feet. People are finding their way into the square. They step out from the seemingly empty arcade that runs right round it, as if by magic. I think for a moment what a deceptive design the square presents: To the eye, it is closed in on three sides, and yet, under those long arcades, it is riddled with narrow

passages from the streets behind. And so, like water to a depression in the ground, people seep into the square from every side, and it is quickly filled up.

Already there are a number of people in costume. When one appears, a circle of picture-hungry photographers packs around it, like pigeons to

60 corn. *As the costume moves slowly through the square, it drags this mass of picture-snappers along with it. Several times I must get up from my stool and make way!*
I escape inside Florian's to warm my feet and hands, and let my watercolors dry. The costumes are of every sort. There is one style that seems to predominate, though: the Ridiculously Ostentatious. I am always wondering what little mind is hiding under all those layers of

gold-and-silver-splashed cloth, sequins, rhinestones and lofty headdress. King for a day! My favorites are those that evoke 18th-century Venice, and I am often amazed by the care to detail that went into preparing them.

A group sits down on the steps of the Café, outside my window. The ladies are powdered and wear décolleté dresses in silk and lace. The men are in wigs and frock coats, sport heeled shoes and canes. They seem to be a theatrical troupe, offering the public a

62

bit of elegant "conversazione" before picking themselves up to disappear again, somewhere, behind the arcades. Then there are the funny outfits. A Turk, a Chinaman, a table laid for dinner. There go a bunch of grapes, a strawberry, a bat, a bull, a bear! A Scotsman in his kilt passes by, completely unnoticed today.

troupes mount the rickety stages set up here and there to perform in traditional costume. There are acrobats, soothsayers, pantomime actors. A number of make-up artists are working along the arcade near the Clock Tower, their palettes of colored greases resting on wastebaskets. Happily, in Venice there is no school today.

Confetti sifts and swirls like snow on the ground. I need a rest. I fold my stool and walk home through silent streets backstage.

I finish my hot chocolate and step back into the square.
The atmosphere in the square is delightful.
In spite of the crowd, there is no rowdiness, but rather a gentle sense of well-being, and of being-here.
A puppet calls out from his booth: The show is about to begin! Theater

Tonight there will be a concert at La Fenice, then on to a ball. And lit by thousands of candles placed the length of it, the Grand Canal will flicker like a constellation pulled down to sleep on the water.

The Piazzetta in winter.

SEASONS

What wind! What rain! I have been attempting to draw the gondola stand outside the Danieli, but it is progressing fitfully between showers of rain. The scirocco has been blowing hard, and has driven the water level high. A wave smacks the underside of the dock I sit on, and a spray of water spits up at me from between the planks. I'm attacked from all sides!

When the scirocco blows in strong like this, it keeps the ebbing tidewater from flowing out. The following tide that comes in has nowhere to go, then, but up: into the streets and houses. Piazza San Marco is the lowest place in the city. As the sea level rises, little pools of water form in the square's depressions, where it bubbles up from drain holes. The water creeps along the paving stones, until it joins another pool, also growing in size. Pigeons and tourists retreat to the few dry islands left in the square, until finally the entire space has been covered, its surface brushed by chaotic sweeps of the wind.

By evening, the wind is stronger than ever. I have been invited to dine with friends in Cannaregio. Unattached shutters slap and bang outside the house, while inside, curtains billow behind closed windows!

Over coffee, we hear the sirens: High water is definitely on the way. We joke skeptically, for serious flooding doesn't occur at this time of year.

Autumn fog, San Giorgio.

But when I depart I am startled to find that the street that brought me here but a few hours ago, is now a canal. I have no choice but to remove my shoes and socks, roll up my trousers, and splash barefoot home. My feet are soon pink with cold, but it is an exciting feeling. The paving stones, which I have known until tonight only under shoe, are smooth and slimy under foot.

In spite of the late hour, the water-filled streets are full of life. There are those like myself, walking home shoes in hand, and others, dressed in high boots, who are out for a stroll. Numerous shops are lit, while all the merchandise is lifted safely out of the rising water's reach. Plastic garbage bags and wooden fruit crates glide along the walls.

The rising tide.
Fishmongers' stalls in Campo Santa
Margherita, winter.

A broken umbrella hurries before me
on bent struts and a wind-filled sail.
I almost regret that my walk is over
upon arriving at my door.
While many would disagree, I cannot
help thinking that it is only right that
we, who visit the sea as it pleases us,
should also suffer visits, as it pleases
her. Certainly, she gives little
warning, and is a nuisance while she
stays, but at least her visits are brief,
if not instructive.

*A disused concrete dock, near the Stazione Marittima. Its flat surface (a rarity
in Venice) makes it the favorite place for roller-skating.*

Beachcombing

*It has been raining, but now it has
cleared. I came for a walk on the
beach of the Lido. The sand is soft
and silky, a warm wind blows in
from the Adriatic, and masses of
clamshells and mussels loll about in
the tepid wavelets at water's edge. In
the shadow of the Excelsior, groups of
tanned boys play football. At the end
of the jetties, a few sunbathers take
in the last golden rays of the sun.
Fat freighters lie lazily on the
horizon.*

*When the sun descends, the air is
bathed in lavender and pink. By eight
o'clock, when I walk back to the
Gran Viale, my only company is the
restful, rhythmic splash of waves.*

The Excelsior jetty, Lido.

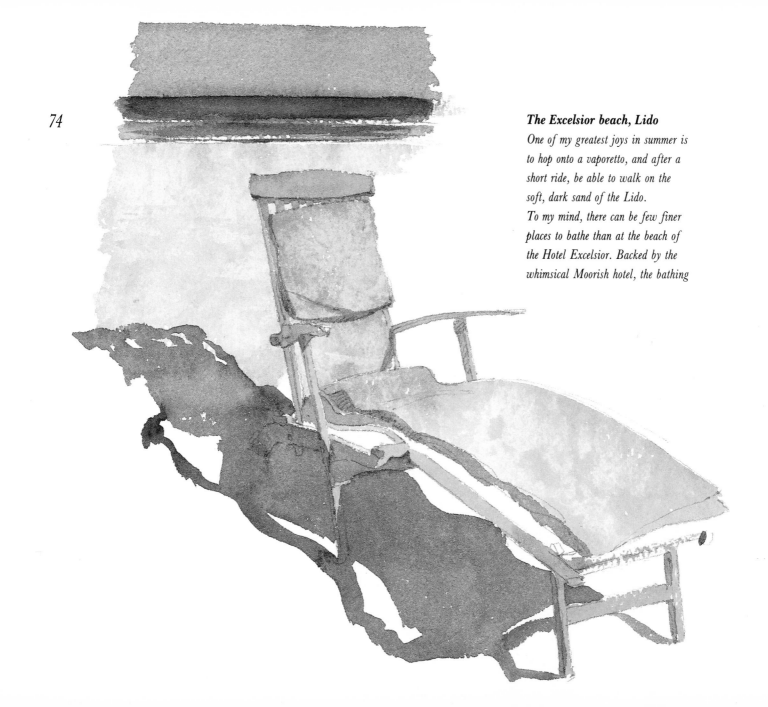

The Excelsior beach, Lido

One of my greatest joys in summer is to hop onto a vaporetto, and after a short ride, be able to walk on the soft, dark sand of the Lido.
To my mind, there can be few finer places to bathe than at the beach of the Hotel Excelsior. Backed by the whimsical Moorish hotel, the bathing

tractors, and in the morning the sand gives the impression of having fallen from the sky, like snow, so evenly it lies. Lawns of grass are laid out between the hotel and the cabins in spring. Lemon and orange trees and bougainvillea vines rise miraculously from tubs buried in the sand. Waiters in brass-buttoned, white jackets glide from the restaurants, bearing trays to the cabins. The air is of times gone by. I love simplicity, but I confess, I like the Excelsior more.

cabins have been arranged in graceful arabesques, providing space and a view of the sea from most of them. Inside each cabin is a table and chairs (for writing, dining, or playing cards) and a wooden bucket of water to remove sand from your feet. A pair of weathered wooden deck chairs stand outside, under the cotton canopy, as well as an extremely soft bed in which to take the sun. At night, the beach is raked by

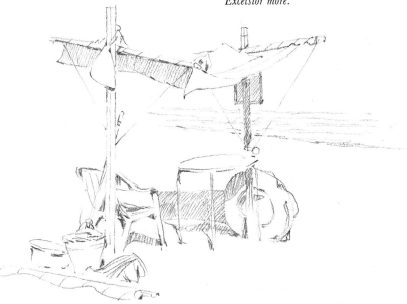

76

Capricious

The weather won't sit still for an hour, and these last days have tested my patience to the limit. No sooner do I begin to work, than it begins to rain, and I haven't been able to start, nor finish, anything. I'm constantly changing my plans to suit what just was the weather.

The newsstand at the foot of Via Garibaldi.

PASSAGES

Now that most cities have traded their street names for those of brave generals and popular presidents, it is a special treat to walk through the streets of Venice and read the stenciled letters on the white "nizioletti," or "little sheets," painted above each calle and campo.

Of course, many streets in Venice carry the names of saints, but they have the merit of telling us we're not far from a church of the same name. And those which do carry surnames nonetheless carry Venetian ones.

But many of Venice's street names conjure up images of an energetic city, teeming with artisans of every imaginable trade. Calle della Fornace: here was once a brickmaker's; Campiello del Tagliapietra: a stonecutter's; Calle dei Fabbri: the blacksmith's; Calle dei Botteri: the cooper's; Calle dei Cerchieri: the hoopmaker's. There is even a Calle delle Carrozze, where a coach-

builder built strictly for an export market. Boat outfitters are remembered in the Calle delle Vele: the sailmaker's. Corte delle Ancore: where anchors were made; Campiello del Remer: the oarmaker's. Rafts of logs were landed at the Zattere: the rafts.

When shopping you'd go to Pescaria for your fish, to Calle Pestrin for milk, to Calle delle Ostreghe for crustaceans. You'd find salt on the

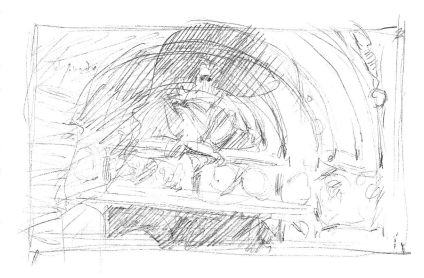

The Arsenal door.

Fondamenta dei Saloni, wine to drink on the Fondamenta del Vin, coal on Riva Carbon, and soap in the Calle della Saoneria. There was Calle del Forno to buy bread, and a Sottoportego del Barbier to trim the beard.

Alas, not even Venice could escape having a Via Garibaldi, but it is revealing that Strada Nova, opened in 1871, was first named Via Vittorio Emanuele... for one year. Then, during the last war, Strada Nova was renamed Via Ettore Muti... for two years. The war over, Strada Nova became Via 25 Aprile... for a few more years. But it was always Strada Nova. Artificial names just don't stick to Venetian "nizioletti."

Arsenal gate

I get very excited by the simple play of light and shadow, like here, at the Arsenal gate. The finely chiselled heraldry on the pillars to the gate presents quite a challenge to draw. This white istrian stone has something magical about it for me. Its surface is always a bit rough, and it vibrates with light in the sun. It has the snap of a crisp sheet, and the dryness of bone. The heraldry in copper sheeting over the entrance also provides an unusual chance to study light on a turquoise ground.

The Arsenal gate.

San Giacomo di Rialto

*At the foot of the Rialto bridge,
tucked behind flower and fruit
vendors, is the little church of San
Giacomo.*

*This is supposed to be the oldest
church in Venice, believed to have been
founded in 421, and restored in 1071.
You can see its small Byzantine dome
as you descend the steps of the bridge,
while its distinctive one-handed clock
and tiny bull's-eye windows overlook
the market.*

San Giacomo di Rialto.

*Flagmast, San Rocco. Every little square in Venice has its flagmast,
from which the six-tailed banner of the Republic flies on holidays.*

Punta della Dogana and Zattere ai Saloni

This is one of my very favorite spots in Venice, especially in winter, where, on a sunny day, against the brick wall, you can finally feel warm. Water sparkles and dances at your feet, and the bleached istrian stone vibrates in the sun.

This building was formerly a depot for salt.

Tugboats resting at Riva degli Schiavoni.

Riva degli Schiavoni

*Save in summer, when it is
unbearably hot and crowded, the Riva
degli Schiavoni remains one of my
favorite walks in Venice.*

*I can't repress a childlike thrill each
time I see the sturdy tugboats lined
up, pressing their big black noses to
the quayside. Ursus, Pardus, Strenuus,
Maximus, Cetus... hairy-chested
machos, all!*

*Perhaps nowhere else in Venice is
there such a feeling of space and air.
Looking out over the wide Bacino,
catching sight of a foreign flag on the
stern of a passing freighter, feeling
the wind blowing in from the Lido:*

Here you know you are on the sea. This quay was not always so wide. I also take a child's interest in finding the little white stone markers embedded in the pavement, indicating the former limit of the quay in front of the buildings.

The last, very colorful buildings to be passed, before reaching the Arsenal Canal, were the "Forni Pubblici" which provided bread for outbound ships from the Arsenal. Beyond the bridge is the Naval Museum, and a little pensione, from whose windows James Whistler drew some delightful etchings of the same quayside.

Newsstand

*From a narrow, compact trunk, this
newsstand opens up in the morning
into a wide, shady umbrella.
Postcards, magazines and newspapers
hang fancifully from its brim. I am
always amazed that everything
displayed outside during the day can
find a place inside the stand at night.*

*Walking behind the altar of S. Giorgio church, these bronze
angels caught my attention: To me, they look like bats!*

Newsstand at the Accademia.

ISLANDS

A morning of rain. Under my umbrella, I sat drawing on the quay skirting the Palazzo dei Camerlenghi at Rialto. This must be the noisiest place in Venice! Coughing, screaming boat engines echo off the underside of the bridge. Captains yell at one another. Horns blare. Porters' carts bang up and down the bridge.

With the weather beginning to look up, over lunchtime I boarded the motonave at Fondamenta Nuova for Torcello. I sat on the top deck, where a chilling wind blew, and from where I could admire towering clouds spreading their shadows over the wide, empty lagoon. There is not much left on Torcello, the first of the island communities. It is said that when the islanders moved on to Venice, they took just about everything here along with them. But the bare essentials have been left behind: There is one canal, a little bridge, a trattoria, a hotel. A church, a museum, a snack stand, and a souvenir vendor.

I followed a path cutting through brush and sea grass behind the church, leading to the lagoon. It smelled dreadful. Dirty kleenex and toilet paper cooked in the sun. And wherever the lagoon met the shore lay a beach of foul litter. Bottles, cans, styrofoam boxes, half-eaten flip-flop sandals, soggy mattresses, a bloated armchair. In such company, I drew the 11th-century campanile.

The coast of Sant'Erasmo, under rain.

Giudecca island.

94

I listened to the wind blowing in the sea grass. A motorboat buzzed somewhere. A fish would plop in the water. And from time to time, a mysterious crunching sound teased me. I would look up and expect to see someone approaching, but each time there was no one around. At last I realized it was just the dead plastic bottles expanding in the sun.

Torcello, the basilica.

A powerful rainstorm blew up over the lagoon and sent me running back to the motonave for Venice.

Massimiliano

I took the vaporetto going to the
island of S. Erasmo. On the way
there, I caught the violent smell of a
garbage barge plying between the Lido
and the mainland. I also saw a man
driving his motorboat in his
underpants.

The first stop on the island is called
Capannone, although there isn't a roof
to be seen anywhere. Just an
arrow-straight, sandy road leading to
the opposite side of the island. Those
who disembarked with me mounted
bicycles and motorbikes, and I was
left to walk the quiet road alone.
Watery ditches lined the roadside.
There was sea grass, heather, poppies,
and wind from the sea. To my right,
between fields of corn, grew the
towers of Venice.

At the end of this road was tucked,
under a fig tree, a vegetable stall.
Lettuce, beans, onions, potatoes,
zucchini and garlic could be bought
directly from the farm. A rooster
called from his coop, leaning against

The Massimiliano, Sant'Erasmo.

Aboard the vaporetto, skirting San Michele.

98

a giant, circular brick fortress in a field, on the other side of the road. This is the "Massimiliano," erected during the Austrian occupation to guard the sea entrance to the lagoon. The road then runs into a grove of acacia trees, and straight into the broad sea channel. Small boats beach here, for there is a primitive canteen, named Bar dei Tedeschi, under the trees. I note that the tables and benches haven't been broken, like at S. Nicolò, on the Lido, just across the channel. Here, they have been cemented permanently into the concrete terrace floor. After drawing, I am happy for the shade of these trees, and for a glass of beer.

The regulars have dispensed with the use of shoes, and also with the use of teeth. But there is a good deal of spitting.

While I don't normally count on locals to get some historical information, I did venture to ask the proprietor's wife, serving my beer, if she knew when the fortress was built. "Hey, Mario!" she called to her husband. "You who was born here, when was that thing outside built?"

Roadside stand, Sant'Erasmo.

Bathhouses at San Nicolò.

S. Nicolò

If the sun is out, any Sunday morning in autumn, winter or spring, we put on our knockabout clothes and board the motonave that plies out to the Lido. Once there, we take a cab to the northernmost point of the island, San Nicolò, where a modest beach canteen remains open throughout the year. The beach here is extensive, and is backed by small, grassy dunes which give an idea of what the whole island must have looked like a little more than a century ago. I love the total contrast to the verticals of narrow, shady streets left behind in Venice. Here, everything is horizontals. Open, wide and bright. A row of pale blue bathhouses, shuttered up for the winter, provide the only windbreak. Some weathered planks leaning conveniently against them provide the means for me to build a small deck in the cold sand.

The canteen, whose sandy terrace is cluttered with beat-up tables and chairs, guarded by a family of tough cats, produces carafes of white wine, plates of crustaceans, and rather plain pasta. We are grateful for the sand at our feet, the view of the sea, the tingling sun on our faces, and wind for the kite. Very simple pleasures. From our position, much of the beach looks as if it were powdered with fresh, white snow. For the beach is covered with shells. I can never quite get over the sheer quantity of them, nor the beauty of their delicate structure and coloring. Crunching underfoot as we walk along the water, I can never resist stopping to pick up a pocketful of these bright little gems, even though I already have a collection at home.

102

Linea mista

At the foot of the Gran Viale of the Lido stand a pair of orange buses bearing the number 11. Once every hour they fire up and depart in tandem on an 18 kilometer-long route to the southernmost point of the Lido islands, the village of Pellestrina.

A ride on Number 11 is always something of an adventure. Since the buses travel together, each one has only to make half the normal number of stops en route to pick up passengers. But when the forward bus makes a stop, it is immediately overtaken by the one behind. Then, as this bus in turn pulls up to a stop, it too is overtaken by the first.

As this comic and incessant overtaking progresses, the speeds accelerate, and tension mounts. It becomes obvious that the object of the game is to see which bus is going to reach the finish line first.

The buses' route is severed midway by a deep sea channel for freighters bound for the port of Marghera. A ferryboat, which gives this bus route the charming nickname of "Linea Mista", stands by to carry us across. The two buses barrel over the loading ramp and switch off their engines, parked, like back at the Lido, one behind the other. But I notice that our bus, which was ahead, is now in second place. During the crossing, there is time for refreshment at the bar upstairs. Mussel farms and fishermen's huts are sprinkled about on the lagoon's surface, dwarfed by ships plowing through the channel, bound for Tokyo, New Orleans or Odessa. Once at the other side, the loading ramp slams down on the quay, and the two buses roar away on the last leg of the route down the noodle-thin island of Pellestrina. Careening around young children and the elderly on bicycles, overtaking each other at every opportunity, it is a miracle that we arrive without incident at our destination. Our driver switches off the engine. We won.

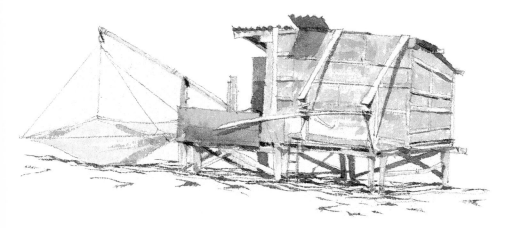

The treeless, sunbaked village of Pellestrina.

Caroman

Alongside the Pellestrina bus stop, a large, white wall runs off into the sea ahead. This is the impressive "Murazzi", a sea wall of fitted istrian stone some 2 1/2 kilometers long and 6 meters tall, closing the lagoon from the sea between the islands of Pellestrina and Caroman. Erected over several decades of the 18th century, it is a well-built piece of masonry.

Looming over the other side of the wall is an unexpected, rusting freighter lying drunkenly on its side. It is a wonderful amount of rusting metal, and I'm surprised no one has come with a blowtorch to recuperate it. But perhaps the Pellestrini are just as happy to leave the ship where it is, as an extra dose of protection against the sea. It should take Nature some time to oxidize it.

A walk along the top of the sea wall reduces the colors of the world to blue. Sea and sky are all one can see.

The sea wall at Pellestrina.

*Halfway out, a lengthy Latin
inscription has been cut in the stones.
The words* Perpetuum, Colosseas,
and Solido *sum it up for me.
The island of Caroman is a tangle of
acacia groves, woods of sea pines on*

*a bed of soft needles, and sand. A
collection of hard-edged bunkers left
from the last war glare in this idyllic
setting.
I can't help thinking how all these
colossal, quiet relics I've seen out here
today, in this empty atmosphere, have
something akin to ancient Egypt:
They will all be here for a long time
to come.
A path through the sea pines leads to
dunes, a wide beach, and the
whitecapped sea. Overlooking the
plastic bottles, oil drums and car seats
washed ashore, here is the wild sand
bar: The Lido that Byron and Goethe
wrote of in their journals. The
cawing of gulls and the splash of
waves is all that can be heard.
There's not a soul in sight.
There is a Robinson Crusoe feeling
about this beach, seemingly at the
edge of the world. And on it, I come
upon a fragile, ephemeral shelter of
driftwood he just might have built.*

The beach at Caroman.

DECKS

My vaporetto has just left, and I wait on the dock for the next one to arrive. My gaze rests on the undulating water, and gradually I become aware of a sorcerer, silently at work around me. Under the arch of a bridge, he is tracing long fingers and quick flashes of light.

On the water's surface, he is swishing and spinning the colors of the sky and the warm facades of the buildings like trails of brilliant wet paint. He is gently rocking the dock I stand on, and he won't allow the horizon to sit still or lie level.

Nearby, he has put a parked gondola to work, rubbing its rope endlessly up and down a mooring post. Beyond, he has aroused the emotions of two resting vaporettos, who, beating their sides noisily against each other, pursue an interminable argument that neither will allow to die.

My boat approaches, and as it bangs against the dock, an impudent wave spits upwards, and just fails to splash me.
I board, and take a seat.

Detail of a gondola.

110

May 17: Vogalonga

This morning, seated with my legs hanging down the stone quayside at the Punta della Dogana, I try to catch, with spare brushstrokes, just a few of the hundreds of oared craft which drift before me in the Bacino San Marco.

It is not without some regret that I look out at these boats. Last year, having just learned Venetian rowing,

I, too, stood in one of them. And if the Vogalonga, or "long row," was the most fatiguing thing I ever took part in, it certainly was also one of the most wonderful.

First organized as a one-shot event to draw attention to the beauty of Venetian rowing, the Vogalonga is now a regular fixture on the Venetian calendar. At nine o'clock, a cannon at San Giorgio signals the departure.

Then, several hundred colorful craft start prying ahead, to the hushed sound of dipping oars, toward the distant islands of the lagoon.

I remember how I struggled to try and keep pace with my fellow oarsmen. Caught in another's backwash, my oar seemed to have a spirit of its own, and kept jumping incorrigibly from the oarlock, to my repeated embarrassment. And I will never forget the exhaustion of three hours of solid rowing. My wrists were as brittle as crackers.

Then, as we re-entered Venice through the Cannaregio canal, we were cheered on by enthusiastic crowds lining both banks. "Alza remi!" ordered our captain. In response to our salute of raised oars there was loud applause. This is a non-competitive event. No one comes in first. But each rower who completes the thirty-kilometer course past Sant'Erasmo, to Burano, Murano, and back, definitely is a winner.

Mooring posts

I had thought of purchasing a small rowing boat, but became discouraged when I began to look for a place to moor it. One would think that in this aquatic town it would be no trouble to tie up your craft, or at least drop anchor. Alas, for all its lack of no-parking signs, I have not known a city more difficult to deposit one's conveyance. The mooring posts you see are all private, and there are no public moorings in town. The driving-in of new pilings is carefully regulated, and is successfully discouraged by lengthy waiting periods

The gondola stand outside the Danieli.

to receive permission to do so.
Having investigated the mooring
situation a bit, I now look at the
poles with some attention. There are
the slender softwood sticks that
gondolas rub against. Heavier craft
get stiff, straight trunks. And then
there are the massive, painted poles
that dip candy-stripes of color into the
Grand Canal. Rarely, if ever in use,
I conclude that their function is just
to look merry.

Vaporetto rope

Hanging casually over the side of
every vaporetto, from a pair of short,
iron horns amidships, is a lanky, pale
blond rope. I always love to watch
this rope perform.
At the approach of a stop, the
conductor will come up and take the
limp thing in both hands. As the ship
pulls up by the dock, he throws the
rope outward, where it catches a
black, H-shaped mooring cleat. Then,

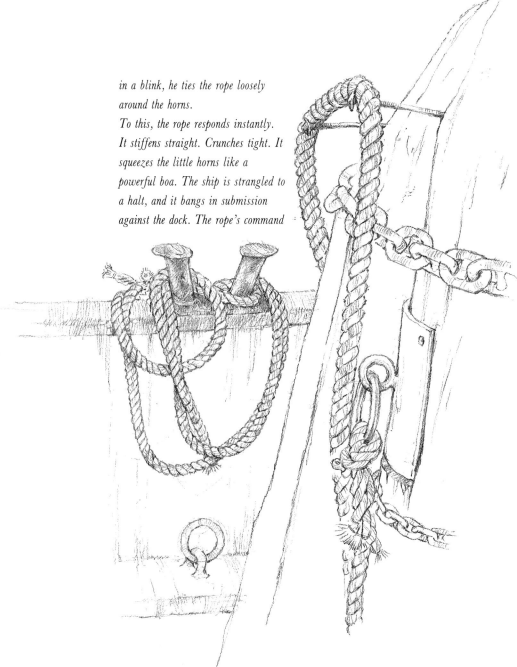

in a blink, he ties the rope loosely
around the horns.
To this, the rope responds instantly.
It stiffens straight. Crunches tight. It
squeezes the little horns like a
powerful boa. The ship is strangled to
a halt, and it bangs in submission
against the dock. The rope's command

is brief, but unyielding.
The conductor then thrusts aside the
boarding gate and, stepping onto the
dock, announces the name of the stop.
The rope, while the conductor assists
an elderly person and parks a
wheelchair on board, remains
resolutely rigid. The gate is half-shut
again but the conductor notices
someone running toward the dock.
"Wait!" he calls to the captain, and
the tardy passenger jumps
triumphantly on board. Thank
goodness, I think; for the next boat
won't come for another ten minutes!
The captain eases his ship gently
back, and the strained rope slackens
with grateful relief. The conductor
gives it a flick, it flies free from the
mooring cleat, and is draped loosely
again over the horns, to rest.
But not for long. The next stop is
already in view.

116

Observed

From my seat on the vaporetto, I watch as another boat passes by. On its deck, I see my barber. He doesn't see me. He is on his way home to Mestre, I think.

You will not find much privacy in Venice. Wherever one goes, there are always acquaintances to be seen, scurrying across a campo, standing in a bar, or waiting for a boat.

When gondolas were a means of transportation, the "felze", the little closed cabin, wasn't just to protect against the weather, but also from curious eyes.

And what I find amusing, as I watch my barber float past, is that at the same time, someone I know could well be watching me.

Clustered pilings and sailing ships on the Zattere.

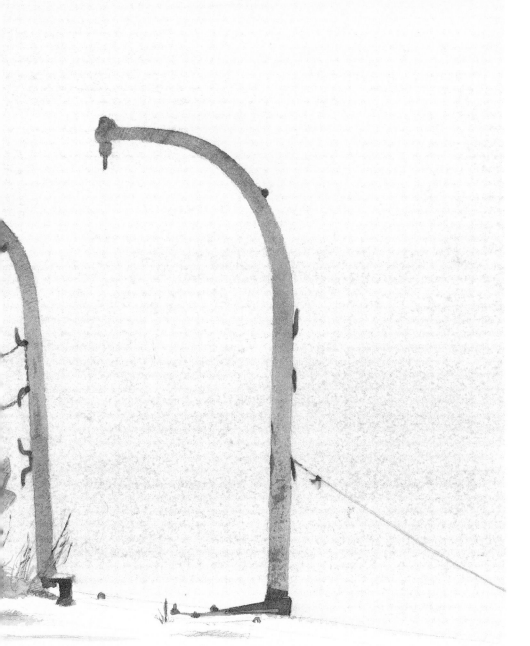

Fog

What snowfall does in other cities,
fog does to Venice.
At such times, like this morning, the
ticket windows for the vaporetto sport
signs announcing: Service Suspended
Due to Fog.
Many vaporettos have no radar.
So many Venetians have no vaporetto.
Fog separates boats distinctly between
the haves and have-nots.
It is not an uncommon sight to see
several radarless boats clinging closely
to the tails of a lucky one that has
got it.

San Giorgio.

July 18: Redentore

I spent the afternoon drawing cats, and then went down to the Punta della Salute to watch the arrival of boats in the Bacino San Marco and Giudecca Canal for the Festa del Redentore.

This festivity, now five hundred years old, is to celebrate the consecration of the church of the Redentore (Redeemer), built at the end of a terrible plague. A floating pontoon bridge is placed right across the wide canal so that pilgrimages on foot can be made to the church, situated on Giudecca island.

But in truth, the festivity is a celebration of summer: a chance to decorate your own boat with Japanese lanterns, leafy canopies, to fill it with food, wine, and friends, watch fireworks, party, and await sunrise on the beach of the Lido.

Gaily colored pavilions, sheltering orchestras, have been erected on barges floating offshore. Atop other barges, long banqueting tables await the arrival of members of rowing clubs, officers, politicians. Crowded fishing boats have come from Chioggia, cargo "peatas" have been filled with relatives. Sunburnt daddies in trunks grill dinner on board.

I had dinner with friends near San

Marco, and we went out to see the fireworks shortly before they were due to begin. But from where to watch? There was a gondola stand downstairs. Someone suggested we rent one. The price was inquired. The reply was outrageous, so we dropped the idea.

A colleague of the gondolier, overhearing us, offered to take us out for half the price – still a hefty sum. We walked on.

"Hey, wait!" he called. "Can any of YOU row?"

"Yes," we replied.

"Then you take ME out!" he said.

I have rowed a few different lagoon boats, but never a gondola. How high one stands on the stern! How heavy the oar! How graceful and slender the craft! I decide immediately that this is the boat for me, and place one foot into the devilish holes in the deck, beside the gondolier's platform. Across the dark and calm water, I push our way among dozens of other gondolas, and station off the Punta della Salute. Suddenly the sky fills with light and thunders with explosions. The fireworks display is magnificent, and lasts nearly an hour. So much explosive is sent

simultaneously into the air, it is as if it were being thrown away, in an effort to be done with it all, once and forever! A rain of rocket paper flutters down ceaselessly. Cinders prick our eyes.

After the display, the gondolier rowed us back... a tricky task amidst the dozens of other boats moving in every direction.

I was to be up early in the morning, so I left my friends and walked home. Under my window, all through the early hours of the morning, glided a seemingly endless parade of boats, passengers weary, lanterns aglow.